BRONC AND BAREBACK RIDING

RODEO

Tex McLeese

The Rourke Press, Inc.
Vero Beach, Florida 32964

PHOTO CREDITS:
© Dennis K. Clark: cover, title page, pages 4, 7, 8, 12, 15, 17, 18; © Texas
Department of Tourism: pages 10, 13, 15; © Pro Rodeo Cowboy Association:
page 21

EDITORIAL SERVICES:
Pamela Schroeder

Library of Congress Cataloging-in-Publication Data

McLeese, Tex, 1950-
    Bronc and bareback riding / Tex McLeese.
        p. cm. — (Rodeo discovery library)
    ISBN 1-57103-344-0
    1. Bronc riding—Juvenile literature. [1. Bronc riding. 2. Rodeos.] I. Title.

GV1834.45.B75 M35 2000
791.8'4—dc21

                                            00–022623

Printed in the USA

TABLE OF CONTENTS

RODEO

Lots of boys and girls love to play cowboy. Some of them love it so much that they never want to quit. When they grow up, they become **rodeo** (ROW dee oh) cowboys and cowgirls. Rodeo is a sport of roping and riding events, the same skills needed during the Old West of the 1800s.

Playing cowgirl or cowboy is fun.

SADDLE BRONC RIDING

This has been called rodeo's "classic" event. It uses the same skills that cowboys in the Old West needed to tame or **break** (BRAKE) a wild horse. The horse was known as a bucking **bronco** (BRON koh). Tamed horses were important for cattle drives. Each cowboy needed as many as one or two dozen horses on the trail. The cowboys who were best at taming wild horses were called **bronco busters** (BRON koh BUS turz).

Cowboys who tame wild horses are called bronco busters.

When teams of cowboys met on the trail or in an Old West town, they would often have contests to see who could stay on the **bronc** (BRONK) the longest. The ride would last until the cowboy was thrown from the horse or the horse had been tamed not to **buck** (BUHK).

Last minute check before the event.

RODEO RIDING

In the rodeo, **saddle** (SAD dul) bronc riding is a timed event that lasts 8 seconds. The event begins with the rider and his horse in a **chute** (SHOOT), behind a gate. The rider starts the ride with his feet over the horse's shoulders. That makes it harder to stay on the horse. When the rider nods to show he is ready, the chute opens. The horse tries to "buck" the cowboy and make him fall off by twisting, turning, and leaping. The cowboy tries to stay on the horse for the full 8 seconds, until the buzzer sounds.

When the rider is ready, the chute opens.

The rider must not let his feet slip from the stirrups.

Cowboys spur the horse with metal on their boots.

RULES

The rider may only hold the horse with one hand on the reins. He loses if he touches the animal, himself, or his saddle with his free hand. He also cannot let his feet slip from the stirrups or drop the rein. He must **spur** (SPUR) the horse with metal on his boots (also called "spurs"). That makes the horse buck harder.

The rider holds on with one hand.

JUDGING

Saddle bronc riding is judged on a scale of 100 points. Half of the points are for the cowboy. Fifty is a perfect score. The other half of the points judge the horse. Fifty points go to the horse that bucks the hardest and makes it most difficult for the cowboy to stay on. Points are taken away if the cowboy doesn't spur the horse hard enough to make him buck.

Judges award points to a skillful rider.

Judges also look at the cowboy's control over the horse throughout the ride. Cowboys also try to be graceful and match their spurring to the horse's bucking. It is very hard for a ride to receive a perfect score of 100. If the cowboy stays on the horse too easily, judges take points away from the horse for not making the ride more difficult.

BAREBACK RIDING

A more recent event, with most of the same rules, is **bareback** (BAYR bak) riding. As with bronc riding, the cowboy must stay on the horse for 8 seconds. He can only use one hand to keep himself from falling off. However, the bareback rider has no saddle or reins. He can only hold the horse with a **rigging** (RIG ging). The rigging is a rawhide handle like the ones on a suitcase. It's attached to a leather strap around the horse's rib cage. With no saddle, the ride is bumpier, more difficult, and more dangerous.

The Casey Tibbs statue at the Pro Rodeo Hall of Fame.

THE MOST FAMOUS RIDER

Casey Tibbs from South Dakota has been called the most famous rodeo rider of all time. During the 1950s, he was a champion at both saddle bronc riding and bareback riding. A 20-foot statue of him stands outside the Pro Rodeo Hall of Fame in Colorado Springs, Colorado.

GLOSSARY

bareback (BAYR bak) — riding without a saddle

break (BRAKE) — tame a wild horse

bronc (BRONK) — short for "bronco," a wild horse

bronco (BRON koh) — a wild horse cowboys ride in a rodeo

bronco busters (BRON koh BUS turz) — cowboys who tame wild horses

buck (BUHK) — leap and twist

chute (SHOOT) — the starting place for riding events

rigging (RIG ging) — rawhide handle for bareback riding

rodeo (ROW dee oh) — a sport with events using the roping and riding skills that cowboys needed in the Old West

saddle (SAD dul) — a leather seat for a rider on a horse

spur (SPUR) — jabbing the horse with metal on boots to make it buck (The metal pieces are also called "spurs.")

INDEX